In Our Neighborhood

Meet a Grocer!

by Becky Herrick

Illustrations by Lisa Hunt

Children's Press®
An imprint of Scholastic Inc.

SCHOLASTIC

Special thanks to our content consultant:

Girvan Williams, Store Manager
Stop & Shop
Stamford, CT

Library of Congress Cataloging-in-Publication Data
Names: Herrick, Becky, author. | Hunt, Lisa, 1973– illustrator.
Title: In our neighborhood. Meet a grocer!/by Becky Herrick; illustrations by Lisa Hunt.
Other titles: Meet a grocer
Description: First edition. | New York: Children's Press, and imprint of Scholastic Inc., 2021. | Series: In our
    neighborhood | Includes index. | Audience: Ages 5–7. | Audience: Grades K–1. | Summary: "This book
    introduces the role of grocers in their community"— Provided by publisher.
Identifiers: LCCN 2021058737 (print) | LCCN 2021058738 (ebook) | ISBN 9781338769869 (library binding) |
    ISBN 9781338769876 (paperback) | ISBN 9781338769883 (ebook)
Subjects: LCSH: Grocers—Juvenile literature. | Grocery trade—Juvenile literature.
Classification: LCC HD8039.G8 H477 2021 (print) | LCC HD8039.G8 (ebook) | DDC 381/.456413—dc23
LC record available at https://lccn.loc.gov/2021058737
LC ebook record available at https://lccn.loc.gov/2021058738

10 9 8 7 6 5 4 3 2 1   22 23 24 25 26

Printed in Heshan, China 62
First edition, 2022

Series produced by Spooky Cheetah Press
Prototype design by Maria Bergós/Book & Look
Page design by Kathleen Petelinsek/The Design Lab

Photos ©: 7: Welgos/Getty Images; 9: Richard Levine/Alamy Images; 11:
Hispanolistic/Getty Images; 13: Jetta Productions Inc/Getty Images; 15: Patti
McConville/Alamy Images; 18 left: Alistair Berg/Getty Images; 18 right: Greg
Baker/AFP/Getty Images; 19 left: FG Trade/Getty Images; 19 right: Krisztian
Bocsi/Bloomberg/Getty Images; 21: Luke Sharrett/Bloomberg/Getty Images;
23: Jacobs Stock Photography Ltd/Getty Images; 25: Drazen_/Getty Images;
31 bottom left: Matt Rourke/AP Images.

All other photos © Shutterstock.

Table of Contents

OUR NEIGHBORHOOD

Hi! I'm Emma. This is my best friend, Theo. Welcome to our neighborhood!

gym

courthouse

pharmacy   bank

The Daily Gazette

local newspaper

Supermarket

supermarket   dentist   veterinarian

salon   movie theater   police station

construction site

4

recycling center

fire station

hospital

restaurant

post office

library

school   CARVER ELEMENTARY SCHOOL

café

Over there is the supermarket. We're making a special birthday dinner for my mom tonight. Theo and I need to go shopping!

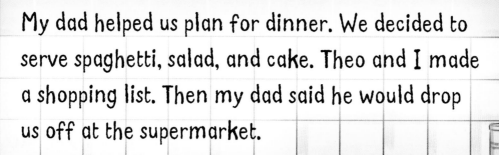

My dad helped us plan for dinner. We decided to serve spaghetti, salad, and cake. Theo and I made a shopping list. Then my dad said he would drop us off at the supermarket.

How will we find everything we need?

Ask the grocery manager for help!

Grocery stores used to be very different! Grocers stood behind a counter. They would collect all the items a customer needed.

MEET MARTIN

We met the grocery manager at the customer service desk. His name is Martin.

We showed Martin our list, and he offered to help us shop. He said we would need to visit several different departments.

I'm happy to do it!

Supermarkets are divided into departments. A different manager runs each department.

Try our Local Products!

GOING SHOPPING

First Martin led us to the produce section. That is where the fresh fruits and vegetables are found.

We picked out lettuce, a cucumber, and a ripe tomato for the salad.

We only sell produce that is ripe or almost ripe.

Produce managers order the types of fruits and vegetables that shoppers want. The managers have to order just the right amount so the produce doesn't go bad.

CUCUMBERS

CUCUMBERS

Next we needed to find the pasta and sauce. "Those will be in one of the center aisles of the store," Martin told us. He explained that stores often put items that you might buy together next to each other.

Tea Coffee 3

We passed the juice aisle on our way to the pasta aisle. We saw a broken bottle—and a puddle of juice—on the floor.

ookies
ackers

Part of a grocery manager's job is making sure the store stays clean and safe for customers.

Uh-oh!

I'll find someone to clean this up.

We found the pasta and sauce. But there were so many options! It was hard to decide what brands to buy.

We looked at the prices and the ingredients. Then we chose a box of spaghetti and a jar of pasta sauce.

This spaghetti looks good to me!

Supermarkets often stock many brands and varieties of the same type of food. They want their customers to have many choices.

Just then another shopper came over. She told Martin that the gluten-free cookies she usually buys were out of stock.

Customer service is an important part of the supermarket business. Managers answer customers' questions and try to make sure they are happy with their shopping experience.

"I'm sorry that we don't have your favorite brand today," Martin replied as we walked to the gluten-free aisle. Then he recommended another brand that was similar.

"How do you keep track of what you have in the store and what you need to order?" Theo asked. Martin explained how products get onto the store's shelves.

Grocers use computer software to keep track of what products are delivered to the store. They track what people buy, too.

Department managers also keep track of what needs to be ordered. This includes getting rid of food that is damaged or expired.

The **grocery manager** places orders to different suppliers to deliver more products to the store.

Trucks deliver the products to the store. There, **clerks** restock the store's shelves.

Cool!

There's a lot to keep track of in a supermarket!

Next we went to the store's bakery. There were so many yummy-looking cakes on display! We picked out a pretty one for my mom.

Can you write "Happy Birthday, Mom" on it?

Bakery managers oversee the store's fresh-baked goods, like cookies and cakes. They often sell specially decorated treats for holidays.

While the cake was being decorated, Martin let us peek through a door into the store's back room. It looked very different from the front of the store!

We just got a delivery.

Wow, look at all those boxes!

Supermarkets usually don't store a lot of extra products in the back room. Workers try to put everything they have out front so it can be purchased!

READY TO PARTY!

We had gotten everything on our list! In the checkout area, we put our groceries on the conveyor belt.

I packed the groceries in my reusable bags as the cashier rang them up. After we paid, we said goodbye to Martin.

It was my pleasure!

Cashiers can tell the prices of items by scanning their bar codes. Cashiers weigh or count produce that doesn't have a bar code. In some supermarkets, customers can use self-checkout to scan their groceries themselves.

25

Back at my house, my dad helped us make dinner.
We used everything we bought at the supermarket.

Theo's parents arrived just as we finished setting the table. We were ready to celebrate my mom's birthday!

This looks delicious!

Ask a Grocer

Theo asked Martin a few questions about his job.

How did you become a grocery manager?

After completing high school, I started out as a clerk at the store. And I worked my way up to manager by doing different jobs over many years! I learned a lot in every job I had at the store.

Do you ever stock the shelves now that you're the manager?

Yes! That's still a regular part of my job.

What is your work schedule like?

I usually get in around 7:00 in the morning. Sometimes I also work in the evenings and on weekends.

What is the hardest thing about your job?

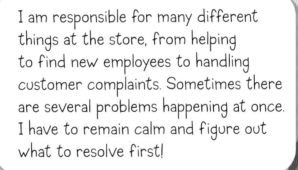

I am responsible for many different things at the store, from helping to find new employees to handling customer complaints. Sometimes there are several problems happening at once. I have to remain calm and figure out what to resolve first!

What is your favorite thing about your job?

I love being able to provide customers with fresh and delicious food and a great shopping experience!

Martin's Tips for Making the Most of Your Shopping Trip

- Bring a shopping list so you do not forget anything you need.

- Try to buy produce that is in season. It will be fresh, so it will taste delicious!

- If you can't find something you're looking for, ask an employee for help.

- Don't forget your reusable grocery bag! In a lot of states, you have to pay for paper or plastic bags. In some places, plastic bags have been outlawed.

- Every package of food has a Nutrition Facts label on it that shows which nutrients are in the food. Comparing the labels on different foods can help you decide which to buy.

A Grocer's Tools

Cash register: Grocers use this machine to charge shoppers money for the items they are buying.

Bar code scanner: Grocers use scanners to keep track of what food is in the store and what is sold.

Robot: Some grocers have robot "assistants" that look for spills or other hazards. Robots can also help keep track of the products in the store.

Loudspeaker: Grocers use loudspeaker systems to communicate with employees and shoppers. Sometimes speakers also play music for the customers.

Index

About the Author

Becky Herrick is a writer and an editor who lives in New Jersey with her husband, daughter, and cat. She loves finding everything on her list at the supermarket!